Photographs:
Front cover
Right hand column: Too often destitution and neglect were the lot of children but this was a spur to social work's beginnings (Museum of Social Work)
Left (Top): A day's outing by horse brake to the countryside might be the only interruption in the bleak regime of the workhouse for its residents (Museum of Social Work)
Left (bottom): The present-day belief in the role of the volunteer brings together the young and the elderly
Back cover
Left: Concern for mentally handicapped people, especially the thousands of children locked away in hospitals, has been a rallying point of the last decade (National Society for Mentally Handicapped Children and Adults)
Right: The plight of the young, race and poor housing and environment are only four ingredients in the problems of inner cities

The Newest Profession

A short history of social work

Dame Eileen Younghusband

The Newest Profession

A short history of social work

Eileen Younghusband

COMMUNITY CARE /IPC Business Press

1981

ISBN: 0-617-00363-7

IPC Business Press Ltd
Quadrant House
The Quadrant
Sutton
Surrey
© IPC BUSINESS PRESS LTD, 1981

Set in 11/11 Times Roman and
printed by Geo. H. Hine & Co, London

The publishers are grateful to Colin Harvey and the Museum
of Social Work, Milgarvie, Dumbartonshire, for permission
to use those photographs credited to them.

Contents

Foreword

Because Dame Eileen Younghusband's life virtually spanned the period covered by *The Newest Profession*, it is at one and the same time a history and a reminiscence. Although it would be misleading to identify her too closely with *all* aspects of social work during the period — even she was not superhuman, though in her sprightly old age she was beginning to create the illusion of immortality — it is certainly true that in social work her influence on policy-making committees at the metropolitan heart of Britain was and is likely to remain unparalleled. Practice, training and the organisation of research owe more to the Younghusband heritage than most practitioners, teachers and research workers can possibly imagine.

It is then a bonus beyond measure for us to have this short monograph as a personal momento of Dame Eileen and as a reminder of her scholarship and her life-long contribution to the social work profession in Britain. Of its kind, it seems to me just right: readable, erudite and never obscure. It stops, as its author acknowledges, "in the middle of a sentence, with no answer to the question whether social work will recover from its indigestion, consolidate its gains and find a more secure identity". Just a hint of bemusement perhaps, a warning that contrary forces may yet destroy the humanitarian ideals that she had striven all her days to safeguard.

Like her history itself, Dame Eileen's life ended in the middle of a sentence; it is for others to determine what the future might bring — to social work, to scholarship and, above all, to the disadvantaged citizens of the world.

Dr Martin Davies
Director, Social Work Programme
University of East Anglia

Introduction

This is a brief account of how social work has come into existence, changed and developed in the past hundred years or so. Its history seems to fall into three distinct stages of advance, inaction, fresh advance, confusion and conflict, yet with consistent underlying threads.

From the beginning social work was interwoven with poverty and deprivation. It changed as conditions slowly improved through the efforts of social reformers, technological advance, the extension of the franchise, the increase of knowledge and changed social attitudes. Extreme poverty grew less but this revealed other persistent social and personal need. Social work remained concerned with deprivation in all its manifestations, with misfits and the "undeserving", and those who for many different reasons could not cope with the circumstances of their lives. Its consistent aim has been to discover how to help such people, though it has had very different ideas from time to time about how to do so. It has been accused, and sometimes accused itself, of being moralistic, authoritarian, knowing best what was good for other people, permissive, soft, manipulative, ineffective, damaging, essential, or a waste of public money. No wonder it has reacted by making too big or too exclusive claims, by being incoherent about what it was and did, and, when it was finally given power, by losing its way.

The 1870s to 1900 —
What the pioneers discovered

Social work was born in the slums of London in the late nineteenth century. Of course it had existed fitfully long before but these were abortive efforts compared with what began to happen about a hundred years ago and finally resulted in social work as a distinctive activity. This only became possible because certain nineteenth century pioneers set forth on an uncharged journey through overwhelming mass poverty, brutality and ignorance and made several crucial discoveries – discoveries that have been built upon and added to in fits and starts ever since.

The first discovery, *knowledge*, was then, as now, bound up with ideologies. Thus the deterrent Poor Law, which cast its sinister shadow over poverty, was ideologically based upon the iron law of wages, the Malthusian theory of population, Benthamism, and later, Darwinism applied to human society. Marxist theories seem to have had little influence at that time. Economics consisted of general theories, so did the nascent sociology, while psychology was almost non-existent. There was thus no testable social science knowledge to underpin practice.

In addition, centuries-old ideas about the absolute rights of the father over his children, and to a large extent his wife, persisted. The philanthropists belonged to their time, particularly in their un-questioned belief in the Protestant work ethic. But they also had a strong Christian motivation expressed in belief in the equality of man, though they did not question the class system and they were more clear about obligations than rights. Their ideal was a society which recognised mutual obligations between rich and poor. This was the ideal that inspired the early social workers and they set about trying to discover how to turn it into reality.

Secondly, there was almost no *usable knowledge* to guide the pioneers other than that based upon direct experience and this was apt to be interpreted in moral terms. But within what became social work three groups of pioneers – Octavia Hill, the Charity Organisation Society (the COS) and the Barnetts at Toynbee Hall Settlement in London's East End – began to keep more or less systematic records, to discuss their experiences and to draw deductions from these. This, with all its limitations, was the beginning that had to be made. It is probably the reason why social work pioneered by this particular group of philanthropists survived and later became a career in its own right with its distinctive practice.

They had to discover more about what makes people tick than

11

comes from individual and often narrowly prejudiced experience, particularly how people who had made a mess of their lives or were overwhelmed by a sea of troubles could be motivated and helped to become independent. Of course this is a never-ending search, of which social work is only a part. Both the religious urge and the prevailing individualist philosophy led the pioneers to concentrate on the individual, on what they called "character", to be supported if it was there or deplored if it was not. In the terminology of modern social work this may have meant "well-integrated" or "inadequate personalities" and "working with ego strengths". On this view, however, poverty and drunkenness were primarily due to lack of thrift, a failure of the moral will, rather than to the iron constraints of social conditions, though the Barnetts — more capable than most of facing reality — urged "with ceaseless persistency that what was wanted was not palliatives for personal suffering but remedies for social disease" (Henrietta Barnett, *Canon Barnett, His Life, Work and Friends.* John Murray. 1918, p. 625).

Thirdly, the pioneers had to discover *social work methods*, "How to do". The COS was undoubtedly the originator of casework, the process of individualising people ("treating the family as a whole", they called it) by thorough enquiry, discovering all the relevant factors in the situation, making a plan with the applicant (we might call it negotiating a contract), giving help adequate to meet the need if help was given, and following the case through. The COS was primarily concerned with extreme material need, with preventing pauperism, eliminating small doles and hand-outs, and encouraging thrift. The method as such, apart from its particular application, had a surprisingly modern ring about it. They divided applicants into deserving and undeserving, an over-simplified and moralistic division later changed to the helpable and unhelpable. The helpable seem to have been those who could surmount a crisis or series of crises with support. The unhelpable fell into the two distinct groups of those who were too demoralised, shiftless or vicious to respond and could only be left to the deterrent Poor Law; and on the other hand those whose needs were so long term on account of ill-health, old age or the like that they were beyond the resources of a voluntary society, and indeed they primarily needed not casework but medical care and social security benefits.

The Salvation Army from its beginnings tried to rescue the "unhelpable" social casualties. And so did the police court missioners of the Church of England Temperance Society whose work in the courts included supervision of offenders, matrimonial conciliation, and also "prison gate" work. (In a later incarnation the missioners were to emerge as probation officers.)

Nowadays we know far more about the complexities of causation, both personal and social, but still too little about prevention or recovery. So the "unhelpable" are still all too obviously with us even in a more tolerant, less judgmental, pluralistic society with its greatly increased knowledge and resources.

So far as methods were concerned, Octavia Hill in her work with tenants, and the settlement movement, led by the Barnetts, discovered much about the value of group discussions, activities, outings and parties, with a small number of members to each helper. But in this country group work remained for a very long time unsystematised compared with casework. What much later was called community organisation and community work was taken for granted by these pioneers. The COS thought that to "organise the district" was more important than casework with individuals. By this they meant the co-ordination of local charities on COS principles but they failed in this, largely because of their own rigidities. In 1894 the Barnetts initiated the Stepney Council on Public Welfare whose "objects included not only the observation and discussion of charity but of all matters affecting the welfare of the district" (*ibid*, p. 633). It was thus a forerunner of the much later councils of social service. Dr Barnardo started workshops for unemployed boys, turned a gin palace into a coffee palace akin to modern community centres, and was driven by the logic of need to provide a number of other resources for the local community. Similarly, Octavia Hill initiated bulk buying for resale to the tenants, trade training schemes, many forms of recreation, and campaigned for open spaces – besides being a founder of the National Trust. Her activities in the housing schemes which she managed interwove casework, group work and community work with each other. In different ways this was taken for granted by the other pioneers. Why the three disastrously fell apart and only casework was conceptualised is a mystery, a failure for which we paid and continue to pay dearly.

These pioneers all believed in treating people as individuals; the Barnetts' motto was "one by one", Octavia Hill thought "knowledge of the passions, hopes and history of people" was crucial. They all spoke of treating people as equals, of friendship and the power of love. Indeed it was this belief, their indignant compassion for the plight of the poor and helpless, which led them to live and work in the appalling slum conditions of the times, to feel the impact of the massive tragedy around them and yet to persist in applying their remedies. It is difficult to understand what equality and friendship could have meant in such conditions of inequality but maybe paternalism was sometimes transcended by mutual recognition that "Judy O'Grady and the Colonel's lady are sisters under the skin". Later, in a more manageable form the concept became making and using a relationship in the interest of the client and within the social work ethical principle of the dignity and worth of the individual. Perhaps elements of what the pioneers sensed is also returning today in rejection of so-called elitism, the rise of more self-help groups and discoveries that consumer satisfaction with social work service depends largely on the social worker's concern about them, dependability, staying on the job, and being "just like a friend". At any rate these pioneers began to discover what was later called social care.

Fourthly, the pioneers had to discover social work itself and *training* for it. It had to emerge from the voluntary friendly or district or charity visitors or settlement residents, or indeed Barnado's beadles or deaconesses, or police court missioners or NSPCC inspectors. The beginnings came when Octavia Hill found she had to train her co-workers, when the COS began to appoint district secretaries (some paid and full-time from 1893) to train volunteers for the actual work with applicants, and when Canon Barnett conducted group discussions and individual searching analyses of motivation with settlement residents. In time some of these different people began to be called social workers.

Training remained for some years a kind of apprenticeship preparation in the work setting, for instance for Octavia Hill's housing managers. The real beginning of education for social work, recorded, transmitted and added to in the light of experience came in 1895 when Miss Sewell, warden of the Women's University Settlement, was instrumental in setting up a joint lectures committee between the settlement itself, the COS and the National Union of Women Workers. The lectures, related to practical experience, were on the Poor Law and charity and almsgiving. "Stress is laid on the practical side of charitable work, numerous instances are cited and the application of the principles of charity explained" (COS annual report 1896, quoted by Marjorie Smith in *Professional Education for Social Work in Britain*. George Allen & Unwin. 1965, p. 21). Later a paid lecturer was appointed, the course was lengthened and more lectures added on "the family and character", "thoroughness" and "personal work". A whole term was devoted to provisions for children. A COS special committee on training said in its report to the council (1898) that "they would like to see in the society the nucleus of a future university for the study of social science in which all those who undertake philanthropic work would desire to graduate" (*ibid*, p. 27).

Fifthly, discoveries had to be made about the kinds of *organisational structure and procedures* through which particular help could be most effectively given. For the COS this meant a central office co-ordinating the work of over 40 district committees all over London. These local offices were easily accessible to applicants and other agencies, while the workers could get to know and be known in the district. The COS central office strengthened and co-ordinated the district offices, conducted enquiries, ran conferences and produced publications which included the quarterly review, annual reports, occasional papers, a cautionary list of fraudulent appeals, pamphlets and leaflets, *How to Help Cases of Distress* and the *Annual Charities Register and Digest*. The value of not only a central office but also local offices covering comparatively small areas has been painfully rediscovered at the present day. The settlement building where residents could settle and not merely visit from a distance and which was a meeting ground for many different people and purposes was highly effective in its heyday.

In the constriction of the settlement movement nothing has been discovered that effectively takes its place. Octavia Hill's system of housing management faded away into technical competence divorced from its social concern. Her permanent contribution lay in the working methods she discovered rather than in her organisational structure. Like other pioneers in the child care field, Barnardo increasingly diversified his provision for children as he gained experience and became ever more adept at money-raising. The range included homes for babies and toddlers, grouped cottage homes with a matron in charge of 20 — 25 girls or boys of all ages in a cottage; reception homes ("ever-open doors") all over the country; several hospital schools for severely handicapped children; a naval training school; a school of printing; apprenticeship schemes; boarding out in country foster homes; and a substantial emigration programme. In addition to this diversification to meet differing needs, Barnardo also discovered the extreme importance of adequate follow-up and after-care. He even saw to a limited extent, as the Barnetts did, that children needed their own mothers who should sometimes receive grants to keep them at home. The only qualified staff were teachers, doctors and nurses and he was blind to the need to train his enquiry staff and the residential care workers.

Thus the pioneers discovered suitable organisational structures for their purposes and the importance of diversification and a range of resources.

These then were five discoveries — and later *social care* — that had to be made and combined with each other to set social work on the tortuous road towards becoming a profession with common trans-missible principles of practice, a code of ethics, a distinctive and recognised training, a body of literature and a professional association.

Of course, there were many more pioneers all over the country than those mentioned here. But it was ultimately the principles of the COS, Octavia Hill and the Barnetts which influenced all the rest, whether here or across the Atlantic. The discoveries were naturally only the beginning: they had to grow and be applied, change and adapt as more knowledge and experience became available, especially as social attitudes changed, the spread of collectivism altered earlier solutions to social problems, and the rights of children began to be recognised.

In time the boundaries of social work expanded in some directions and contracted in others. They expanded to include residential social work (wholly neglected until well into the twentieth century), group work in many different situations, education welfare and some forms of community work. The boundaries contracted from housing management, youth employment, personnel management, and educa-tion in its more formal sense. Yet education was the heart of the matter to Octavia Hill and the Barnetts who believed that music, drama, the arts and enjoyment of nature should be made freely available to the poor because "the religion of enjoyment" was the best cure for the dreary apathy of their lives.

The clash of social attitudes at the end of the nineteenth century underlay the conflict between the COS and Sidney and Beatrice Webb. The COS leaders, Charles Loch, Helen Bosanquet, Octavia Hill and others believed in the necessity for an essentially deterrent Poor Law, though relief if given should be adequate. They thought, in the face of overwhelming evidence, that the poor could by thrift and prudence and with the help of relatives, friends, neighbours and employers live independent lives and save against ill-health and old age. They opposed all forms of state financial provision, for example old age pensions or school meals, on the grounds that these would pauperise and undermine incentives to work. The Webbs on the other hand pointed out the inefficiency of the deterrent Poor Law which could take no action to prevent destitution or to set people on their feet again. They also knew at first hand the degrading poverty of slum areas in big cities which had grown up as a result of the industrial revolution, the insanitary houses in which all ages and both sexes might sleep in the same overcrowded rooms, the poorest be half starved in their ragged clothes, the children bare footed in all weathers, and disease, ill-health and early death taken for granted. Some steady employment at a decent wage existed but alongside sweated industries, casual and seasonal labour and unemployment caused by trade cycles. There was much child labour until the education acts from 1870 onwards finally provided the solution. Hours of work were long, much unskilled work was monotonously soul destroying and holidays with pay lay far in the future. It was not surprising that men and women aged prematurely, that many found drink the easiest escape and that unremitting thrift was too austere a virtue. The Webbs and others, including the Barnetts, realised that moral failure lay primarily with employers of sweated labour, slum landlords, supine local authorities and the ignorant rich. They saw the remedy in collective action against collective ills, such as extending and enforcing housing, health and conditions of work legislation, instituting school meals, and the decasualisation of casual labour. These claims were reinforced by the findings of Charles Booth's great enquiry, conducted from Toynbee Hall, into the *Life and Labour of the People of London* which began to appear in 1883. This survey showed to everyone's surprise not the submerged tenth which had been expected but that 35 per cent had only the barest necessities, of whom nine per cent fell below even that minimum. This revelation greatly strengthened the case for collective action.

So far as the emergence of social work is concerned, the significance of the COS-Webb controversy was that it began to clarify those ills which only large-scale public action could remedy, ills which could not be eliminated by social work with individuals. Social work still

16

continues to be used inappropriately in such circumstances, though the dilemma remains that people who are poor or ill-housed or over-burdened cannot be left unhelped because the long-term remedy lies elsewhere.

1900 -1945 —
A long standstill
then fresh activity

In the first decade of this century Toynbee Hall continued to inspire social research, notably Beveridge's study of unemployment which shifted the problem from the worker to the organisation of industry; and the enquiry into sweated industries which resulted in statutory wage-fixing machinery. There was no break in Sidney and Beatrice Webb's massive studies which produced evidence of neglected social ills and suggested remedies.

The 1905–09 Royal Commission on the Poor Laws included Charles Loch, Octavia Hill, Helen Bosanquet and Beatrice Webb. The COS leaders and others signed the majority report, Beatrice Webb and her supporters the minority report. The majority recommended retention of a much-modified Poor Law which would yet still have had the stigma of pauperism attached to it. The minority report recommended the complete break-up of the Poor Law and the substitution of a series of specialised services for unemployment, health and education. The proposed abolition of the Poor Law with all the profound hurt and suffering it had inflicted was undoubtedly right but in some ways the majority showed a greater understanding of human need. If they could have shed their pauper blinkers and recommended that a new type of personal social service should be slid into the old structure we might have had a Seebohm reorganisation 60 years earlier and with less upheaval.

One reason why this would have been historically impossible concerns another element in the voyage of discovery, one which the pioneers sometimes stressed but whose absence partly accounts for the early twentieth century stagnation. This sixth discovery was *social care* or the personal social services (unfortunately we have no satisfactory term for it in the English language). It was based on realisation that individuals of any age must grow and be sustained as whole people if they are not to atrophy or become distorted as persons. Charity had become identified with judgmental parsimony, welfare was substituted for a time but savoured too much of sentimentality or paternalism. A clear concept of social care was missing. Beatrice Webb in particular failed to see that "the naughty boy, the homeless and neglected child, the unhappily married, the neurotic invalid, are clearly not problems in isolation but partly at least the product of the problems of some home" (Una Cormack, *The Welfare State*. The Family Welfare Association. 1953, p. 33).

18

This myopia was equally great in all forms of residential care where, apart from nurses and teachers in their special roles, either untrained motherly women or good disciplinarians were thought to be adequate to the social care, nurture or control task for people of any age in any kind of total institution. Clearly, many individual staff gave personal care and nurture but it was not institutionalised.

Initiative and fresh discovery died down in social work itself for almost the first 40 years of the twentieth century. Yet tremendous social changes took place and the world of the 1930s was far different from that of the 1900s. The creative pioneers had somehow failed to disentangle social work as a relevant form of practice to meet social need from an outmoded ideology. And when they themselves retired or died no second generation of leaders more attuned with the times but with their force and zest, indeed with their influence in the corridors of power, succeeded them. As a writer in the 1930s put it: "Much of their work is out of print and out of date. Where are their successors? Where are those who, inheriting from them ideas and standards which bear the test of time, can interpret them to a generation which speaks a different language and moves in a totally different environment?" (Elizabeth Macadam, *The New Philanthropy*. George Allen and Unwin. 1934, p. 21).

The great advances came from other directions, embodied in social legislation that included school meals for children "unable by reason of lack of food to take advantage of the education provided for them", school medical inspection and treatment, secondary education, juvenile courts, protection of neglected children, old age pensions (and later benefits for the unemployed, the sick, orphans and widows), trade boards with compulsory powers to fix wages in certain sweated industries, labour exchanges, and better public health provision. Appropriate remedies were thus introduced for ills which the COS had previously thought should always be individually investigated by social workers. A balance so disastrously lacking earlier thus began to be redressed through large-scale public services but social workers were either not employed in them or else thought only marginally relevant. Almost the only exceptions were hospital almoners in voluntary and a few municipal hospitals, and untrained police court missioners. The Probation of Offenders Act 1907 and the later Criminal Justice Act 1925 first permitted and then required the appointment of probation officers paid from public funds to "advise, assist and befriend" probationers. Social workers were not employed by local authorities largely because these recruited staff (other than professionals) in their 'teens and they rose by promotion and learning on the job.

Promotion prospects for social workers were almost non-existent for many years and even by 1939 most salaries ranged from about £150 to £400 a year. Most social workers, whether trained or untrained, were employed in voluntary family welfare agencies (mainly giving financial help), in the Invalid Children's Aid Association, and as moral welfare workers. The strong concentration on relief-giving and morality was thus still apparent. Over the years a number of gifted people came into social work with or without training. Some became head almoners, principal probation officers, secretaries of voluntary organisations, settlement wardens, or London County Council school care organisers, or else joined the staffs of university social study departments. They did not make the discoveries nor exercise the influence of the early pioneers and they stopped short of recorded and pooled experience but they learned a good deal about social need and how to meet it with the resources available and about individual crises and disabilities.

Probably there was more concern about housing, about over-crowding, slum clearance, better standards and rent restriction than almost any other social need, especially after the First World War when over a million houses were built in a few years with more generous grants. Large housing estates and satellite towns spread and by their lack of civic amenities, shopping centres, meeting places and good transport, indeed blindness to the social dimensions of welfare, generated problems which still continue.

Unemployment was the crucial problem in the depression years of the 1930s. The local authority structure and resources were wholly inadequate in the distressed areas. The many clubs and social centres for the unemployed, largely initiated by the National Council of Social Service, helped to alleviate the personal and social rot of unemployment but could not touch its economic causes. The Poor Law guardians were abolished in 1929 and their functions transferred to the county and county borough councils who were to operate through public assistance committees. Many Poor Law hospitals were transferred to the public health committees. But the dead hand remained in the public assistance services.

Social work did not progress either during or as a consequence of the First World War. And the necessary discoveries all languished. The first, *knowledge*, derived from research rather than broad theory advanced unevenly: there were several social surveys and studies of poverty which extended Charles Booth's and Seebohm Rowntree's earlier surveys. But sociological and psychological action research studies were lamentably lacking. The general text books on psychology did little to illuminate the varieties of human experience, while neither psychoanalysis, Piaget's research, nor Watson's behaviourism made much impact. The careful studies of the cultures of Asian and African peoples had no counterparts for this country. A coherent infra-structure was missing, the knowledge which could be applied to form a basis for social work practice.

Thus the second necessary discovery, *usable knowledge*, did not advance though much that existed was not applied. The kind of eager enquiry and action which characterised the pioneers was lacking and British social workers settled down to learn from little but their own experience and the policy of the agency. Even the practice wisdom which resulted from this was not recorded, systematised, tested and transmitted. The third necessary discovery, *method*, "how to do", consequently languished. The original close relation between casework, group work and community work, so characteristic of the aims and activities of the pioneers, was broken. Agencies became more specialised and only casework was identified as distinctively social work. There was much work with groups, whether in youth clubs or the many other clubs which were one of the few creative responses in the depression years. The National Council of Social Service (now the National Council of Voluntary Organisations) and local councils of social service were active in community work in the inter-war years. But none of this was conceptualised. There was no theory to which it could be related and the impulse to distil theory from the experience of practice was lacking.

The first real breakthrough in the development of method came with the publication in the USA of Mary Richmond's *Social Diagnosis* (1917). This was the result of a long process of conceptualisation from many records in which she came to see "the treatment of individuals as a total process, the techniques of which could be ordered, described, analysed and transmitted from one generation of social workers to another". (Kathleen Woodroofe, *From Charity to Social Work*. Routledge & Kegan Paul. 1962, p. 105). The processes of casework included study of the facts, diagnosis of the problem and plan of treatment. She believed in the equal importance of advances in the welfare of both the individual and society — a balance subsequently lost. In spite of its limitations of too great detail for actual practice, Mary Richmond pioneered the advance which social work had to make if it was to begin to emerge as a profession which could be practised in any agency — or independently. It is doubtful whether she directly influenced social work practice in this country. She formulated the framework into which new concepts from dynamic psychology were incorporated from the 1920s onwards in the USA. These changed the focus from environmental needs to the dynamics of personality, to internal motivation rather than the individual passively acted upon by environmental factors. Social workers absorbed from psychoanalysis the concepts that every psychic event has a history rather than just happening at will; that unconscious motivation aims at the fulfilment of basic human drives; and that family relationships are crucial in their effects on personal development.

These dynamic concepts seemed much more relevant to social work practice, to the understanding of apparently irrational and self-destructive behaviour, than the rather arid intellectualism of previous psychological theories. They shifted practice from emphasis on economic and sociological factors in individual and family life, and the small family group emerged as the first and most potent influence on attitudes. The consequence was that some American social workers became more interested in the internal dynamics of individual behaviour than the influence of the social environment, economic factors and cultural attitudes. But later by slow degrees the significance of the complex interaction between the two was recognised.

The fourth discovery, *training*, continued to develop in the first few years of this century. In 1901 the COS set up a broadly based committee on special education with a number of academic members. Its aim was to plan lectures closely related to practical work in different parts of the country. The Liverpool School of Social Science was started in 1904 jointly between the university, a settlement and the Liverpool COS. Other schemes followed, and in 1903 the COS itself started its school of sociology in London. This provided a two year full-time course with Mr (later Professor) Urwick in charge. He thought it was necessary for practitioners to be well instructed in methods based on science and practice on principles. But social workers were still in the rule of thumb stage, following customery methods without knowing whether they were good or bad. The curriculum had in it elements of social theory, and administration, including economic theory, social and industrial history, sociology, social philosophy and the principles underlying social work. There were substantial periods of practical work in various social agencies. Unfortunately no information exists about the actual content of any of these lecture courses, though their titles would be familiar today. In 1912 the school of sociology was amalgamated with the social science department at the London School of Economics on the understanding that its work would be carried on under Professor Urwick. This continued for a time but then social science teaching and academic impatience with the demands of practical work both increased until by the 1920s there was only a tenuous relationship between the first rate social science and social policy teaching and unrelated practical experience with little educational content. The structure pioneered by the school of sociology was thus dismantled and lost. The COS froze in an out-moded pattern, while the universities eschewed vocational training.

This gap in social work education continued until 1929 when the mental health course was started at LSE on a pattern copied from the United States which much later became the basis of all education for social work in this country. It was a small specialised course for psychiatric social workers, financed by the Commonwealth Fund of America. It consisted of lectures by psychiatrists, psychologists and social workers, together with practice under teaching supervision to relate it to theory. The products of this course were regarded as advanced practitioners compared with those who took the other, often narrowly technical courses which inevitably grew up when the sometimes excellent social science courses did not aim to produce students with some competence in practice.

There were no training grants for students, which is one reason why few men trained and why social science departments were forced mainly to recruit middle class young women. The one remarkable exception was the Home Office decision in 1936 to award fees and maintenance grants for probation students to take a social science course and probation training. The first publicly financed training council, the Probation Training Board, was set up to guide the scheme.

The fifth discovery, *organisational structure and procedures*, made little progress and management studies were non-existent. An important innovation was the inspection of probation officers by the Home Office. Later, the Children's Branch of the Home Office inspected approved schools and some children's homes. This type of inspectorate became in time a standard-setting, information-sharing, advisory and consultative service. This was also one element in the slow and uneven growth of a partnership between public and voluntary agencies which at its best was a real discovery of the twentieth century.

Almoners, probation officers and some psychiatric social workers were employed in agencies whose primary purpose and professional expertise were not social work. Social workers thus had to discover how to make an effective contribution in interdisciplinary situations. This was long in coming.

The sixth discovery, *the social care function*, made little progress before, during or after the First World War and had not been clearly identified by 1939. But it was coming near the surface, for instance in the progressive schools of the 1930s, the Caldecott Community, the Methodist-inspired National Children's Home and Barnardo's new training schemes for residential staffs, and some work with young delinquents.

At the outbreak of the Second World War there was mass evacuation of school children, mothers with small children and later those made homeless by air raids. But the arrangements were inadequate and the human factor had been largely ignored; for instance children who remained with their mothers in air raids suffered less than those who were evacuated without them. In many areas local authorities were quite unable to cope with the size and range of evacuation problems, with the many misunderstandings between the evacuees and their hosts, the sheer shortage of equipment of every kind from nappies to large houses for groups of children. In time hostels for "difficult" children, for mothers and infants, school camps, mothers' clubs, occupational centres and so on were started. In the blitzed areas it was not only a question of services to rehouse the homeless but also to alleviate for them and others bewilderment and the shock of loss. Thus the social dimension, still called welfare, began to be identified by its manifest absence. "This development . . . was part of a much wider movement affecting not only the post-raid services. Until 1940 trained and experienced social workers had been generally ignored by government departments. But after 1940 the situation changed completely. The value of trained staff, from almoners in hospitals and clinics to social workers engaged on psychiatric work, child care and family casework, rose in official esteem. There followed something approaching a famine in social workers" (R.M. Titmuss, *Problems of Social Policy*. HMSO and Longman. 1950, p. 289).

The hostels for "difficult" children, those who stole, were bed-wetters, ran away and were generally unruly, were started in 1940 to prevent another angry wave of protests from householders in reception areas. "Many became dumps for all kinds of rejected children" (*ibid*, p. 379); and: ". . . All kinds of people, shading from the very good to the very bad, were appointed as wardens and matrons" (*ibid*, p. 386). Gradually the service was reorganised, the hostels were classified, there was some staff training and psychiatric advice and treatment was provided.

In mid-1940 social workers were appointed as Ministry of Health regional welfare officers to deal with evacuation problems and shortly afterwards welfare inspectors were added to help with difficult re-housing cases and to act as the eyes and ears of the London regional organisation. "They were needed because they knew about people and about distress, because they could help to bring the wide array of statutory and voluntary agencies to bear on the several needs of a particular individual at a particularly urgent point in time, and because they were qualified to report in practical terms on the way in which one service reacted on another and on the people needing help." (*ibid*, pp. 289–90). A 1940 Ministry of Health circular said: ". . . the re-housing of homeless people involves more than securing simply that there is accommodation . . . for the number of persons involved. Casework, taking into account the needs of the individual persons or families affected is also necessary . . .". In quoting this circular (p. 290) Titmuss went on to comment that social workers' contribution to solving homeless people's personal problems was valuable in itself and "because it expressed almost a new concept of the relationship between public agencies and the public served" (*ibid*, p. 290). The personal social services, social care, was coming to birth.

The Ministry of Health encouraged the employment by local authorities of experienced social workers to develop welfare provisions for evacuees and homeless people and to match special needs with special provision. Similar appointments were advocated in the bombed areas. By the end of the war 70 local authorities had appointed social workers. These were in addition to the Ministry of Health's welfare officers and the social workers of the Provisional National Council for Mental Health and other voluntary organisations.

The citizens' advice bureaux were started in 1939, largely staffed by volunteers but with some casework and good back-up services. From 1940 the Pacifist Service Units were trying to discover how to help, support and change "problem" families. They worked in teams and carefully recorded their work. After the war as the Family Service Units they continued in the forefront of progressive social agencies.

The occupational therapy department of Barnhill Poor House (now Foresthall Hospital), in about 1910. It was built nearly half a century before for 2,000 · inmates (Museum of Social Work)

Concern, interest, friendship . . . the craft shop in a present-day children's home

18 – 26 Stepney Causeway, East London, headquarters of the Institutions and Boys' Home, a street where Dr Barnardo set up headquarters (Museum of Social Work)

Volunteer befriending is part of a modern intermediate treatment scheme . . .

. . . but the harsh, prison-like regime of Send Detention Centre shows another way of dealing with the recalcitrant young in the 1980s

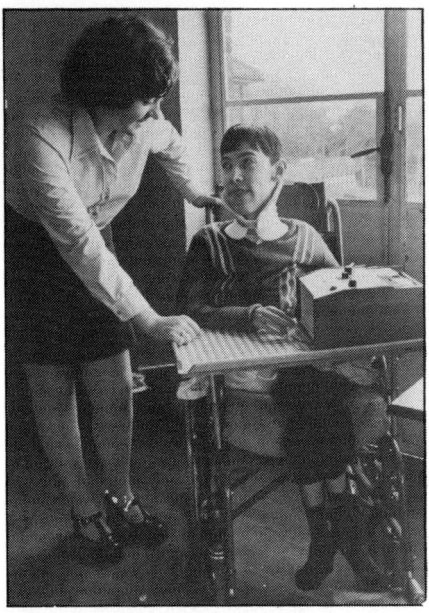

The National Listening Library

Two children who found a home th

Child abuse . . . the NSPCC appeals

The growing numbers of elderly people

...ative, modern adoption schemes

Lady Bountiful has vanished in today's volunteering

...enge to social work and society

Homeless youngsters – A Church of England Children's Society project

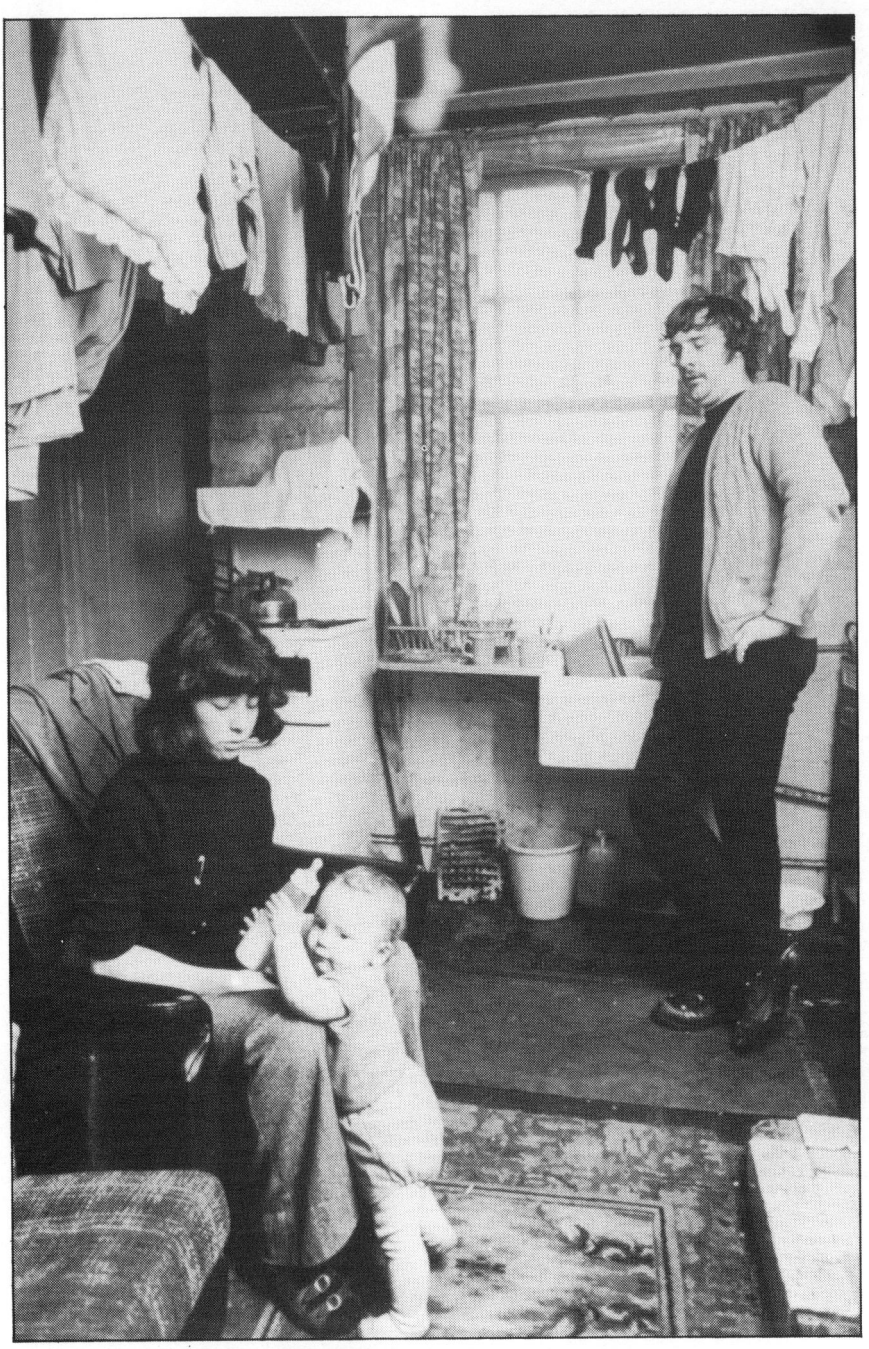

Home in Britain 1981 — what hope for the child and his parents?

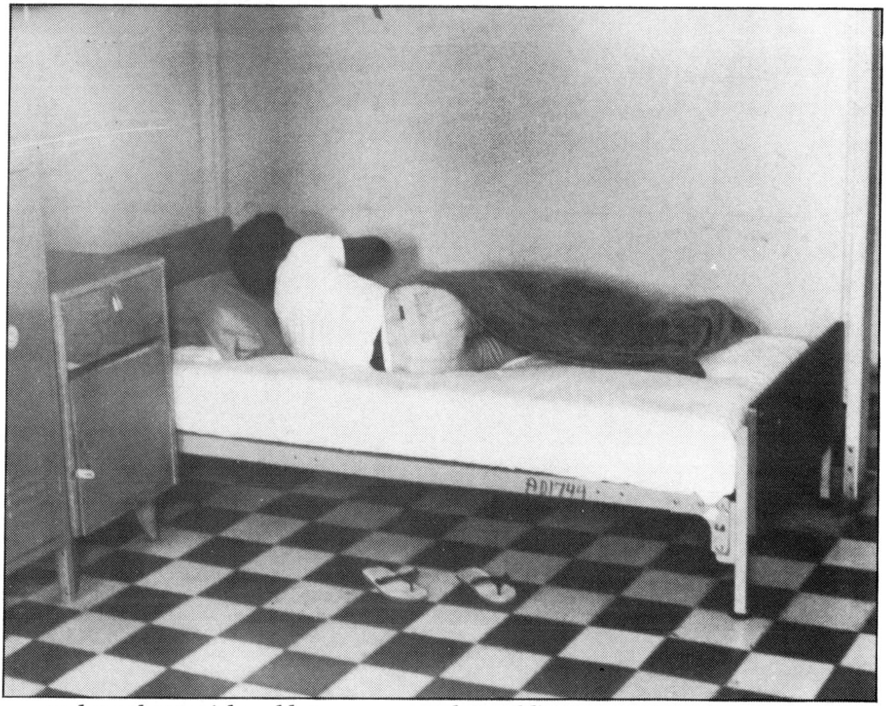

. . . and another social problem – a young drug addict in a treatment centre

A windowless room and inhabitant in 1930 (Museum of Social Work)

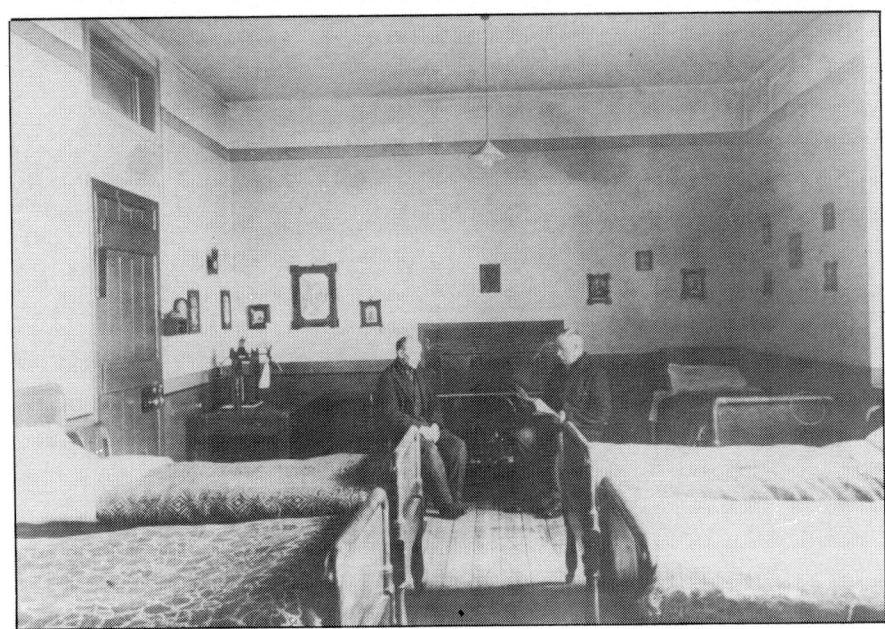

The despair of the single homeless, low in official priorities

Two elderly workhouse inmates in 1910 (Museum of Social Work)

The regional services of the Provisional National Council for Mental Health, with psychiatric social workers in charge, helped people suffering from war neuroses. Civilian resettlement units were set up under government auspices at the end of the war, directed by psychiatrists and with social workers on the staffs, to help returned prisoners of war to adjust to freedom in a changed society.

The Beveridge report (1942) inspired a long-forgotten euphoria with its logically argued plan to abolish the five giants of want, squalor, ignorance, unemployment and ill-health; and to give financial security "from cradle to the grave". Thus fluttered those social work dovecots where relief giving was still their stock in trade who feared that "Beveridge would kill social work". They were wrong because the Beveridge report was never fully implemented and because they failed to realise that social care was something much broader than financial help alone.

The Curtis report (1946) on children deprived of a normal home life showed up the administrative chaos of services divided between four different authorities and the same number of government departments and inspectorates. The committee's comments on children's leisure, supervision, toys, upbringing, their concern for individual chidren's happiness and development, were worlds away from similar descriptions in the late nineteenth century. In the Curtis report there was a realistic and imaginative understanding of the needs of children, and their actual care was judged in the light of this. So the importance of social care was recognised in relation to one type of residential situation, though it was a long time before it spread to those for adults.

1945 to the 1970s —
Growth and dissention

War-time experience established for the first time that social work was a necessary function. This meant trying to close the gap between perception of the task and performance, a never-ending struggle in which more knowledge revealed more complexities and ideologies clashed.

Education was vastly extended in 1944 and family allowances were introduced. In 1948 the welfare state came into existence with the National Health Service, an increased range of national insurance benefits, nationally paid assistance allowances, abolition of the Poor Law, extended housing provision, reform of the penal system, residential and other provision by local authorities for old and handicapped people and some homeless families; and most important of all for social work, the Children Act which instituted a unified public service for children deprived of a normal home life by creating local authority children's departments and the profession of child care officer.

Social workers advanced very unevenly in these different services. For the first time they began to be employed in large numbers in local authorities. This was primarily in the child care service but local authority officials who learned on the job, might not keep case records and had no common standards continued to be the backbone of the health and welfare services until the 1960s. In the public services other social workers had to face, as probation officers had long done, the dilemma of exercising control as well as care functions and working within a framework of regulations where in some circumstances they might have to use compulsion. To some social workers care and control were part of the same continuum, to others they were irreconcilable.

Some voluntary organisations experimented and campaigned on behalf of particular groups. But others with set ideas from the past took a long time to move successfully into the changed second half of the twentieth century. Many more self-help and pressure groups sprang up but the whole idea of participation, that consumers should have a say in how services were provided only emerged by degrees.

The shortage of qualified social workers was revealed by every government committee of enquiry into particular services. It took some time for appointing committees to realise that trained social workers could do a better job with more consistent standards than local people with a warm heart or ability to make the wayward conform. It was particularly difficult to accept that the art of human relationships could be improved by training. But training began to be assumed for any skilled job. In many directions earlier assumptions clashed with the new world of the second half of this century.

The old COS emphasis on the importance of the family revived in the light of fresh experience, particularly in the child care service. But services were specialised, there was overlapping, serious gaps and departmental rivalries — indeed a situation which the 1909 minority report had not foreseen. In the 1960s a demand arose for a family service, a demand which however different and more generous its form, should have delighted those who signed the 1909 majority report. The final outcome of this pressure was the 1968 Seebohm report on the personal social services which went far beyond a family service and resulted in a reorganisation that amalgamated the children's and welfare services. The similar Scottish enquiry and reorganisation also brought in the probation and after-care service.

The professional associations of probation officers, medical social workers, psychiatric social workers, child care officers, moral welfare workers and others continued until all except that for probation came together in 1970 to form the British Association of Social Workers.

Social work in its various settings developed a practice wisdom based on experience but not tested by research, indeed there was increasing lament about the lack of social work research, although the amount of social work writing steadily increased so that we ceased to rely exclusively on American material. Studies on either side of the Atlantic of social work effectiveness generated violent controversy. Enquiries into consumer reactions only began in the 1960s: they showed that satisfaction was related to frequency of contact, relevant service and manifest desire to help. There was a vast difference between Barbara Rodgers' survey of social work in a northern town in 1958 (*Portrait of Social Work*. Oxford University Press. 1960) and those of Olive Stevenson and Phyllida Parsloe (*Social Service Teams*. HMSO. 1978) and E.M. Goldberg and William Warburton (*Ends and Means in Social Work*. George Allen and Unwin. 1979). The first demonstrated the consequences of social work based on purely personal responses, lacking standards of practice, training, consistent aims and a theoretical underpinning of general policy. The later studies showed that these were assumed but with a disappointing failure, partly for organisational reasons, to utilise them fully. The result was uneven patterns of service for different categories of client, constant response to crises but too little selective, thorough or preventive work, and unfaced problems of generic versus specialised practice.

Welfare assistants and trainees and other ancillary staff were only clearly differentiated (in theory if not in practice) from social workers in the 1960s. The valuable complementary functions of volunteers only began to be clarified in the 1970s, with the need for recruitment, training, matching and support services to make their contribution mutually rewarding to them and their clients. Many self-help groups also needed social work and other support services, and in their turn might forestall the need for social work help to individuals. The increase in ethnic minorities made it essential for social workers — and others — to learn about their different cultures, values, habits and expectations.

Community work had long been practised in settlements, councils of social service and other settings but it only began to be identified as such in the late 1960s. It included helping local groups to come together to work for something they wanted (or to prevent something they didn't want), and to acquire the necessary social skills and resources, i.e. to gain more power over circumstances and to bring about desired change. Social surveys, social action, inter-agency co-operation and social planning were all part of community work.

These examples of developments in the decades after the Second World War show that new ideas, methods, attitudes and services were all struggling with old ways and attitudes but only really began to come to fruition in the 1960s. The six necessary discoveries made richer and more varied progress in this third period than in either of the others so that what follows can only be brief illustrations.

The first discovery, *knowledge*. In the late 1940s only one social science department had a research unit, but some relevant research was undertaken by other departments or outside projects financed by trusts. Most advances in knowledge came from the United States until the situation began to change from the 1950s. The new discipline of social administration also began to add to knowledge relevant to social work. Developments in economics, anthropology, demography, biology and medicine were increasingly significant, though the major contributions of general and usable knowledge came from psychology and sociology.

Economic and sociological studies of poverty made it clear that only large-scale change could deal with structural causes. Yet even if poverty and bad housing were eliminated there would still remain among all classes many complex factors, whether or not preventable, that contributed to social and personal distress. The increase of both knowledge and conflicting theories was so great in this period that knowledge and usable knowledge far exceeded its actual application.

Second, *usable knowledge*. In the post-war years there were many complaints that social science students were being taught abstruse economic theory, sociology that did not make social structure and institutions significant in practical terms, and academic or experimental psychology irrelevant to understanding human behaviour (as though the proper study of mankind was not, as has been said, man but rats). This was only partly due to lack of usable knowledge. A change began with the publication of Bowlby's *Maternal Care and Mental Health* (World Health Organisation. 1951) which demonstrated by clinical studies the infant's need for consistent mothering. This reinforced war-time evacuation experience and helped the new children's departments to develop a theory of practice. Concurrently psychoanalytic theory was making a major impact on casework method; while anthropological studies were demonstrating the effect of different cultural values and behaviour on patterns of family and social life. Role theory began to be applied in social work understanding and thus bridged a gap between sociology and personality development. Later, developments in learning theory led to use of a behaviour modification in some social work practice, using concepts of positive and negative reinforcement.

Stress, separation, deprivation, alienation and loss emerged as major factors in need for social work help and therefore the importance of usable knowledge about precipitating factors and how to forestall, detect and compensate for these, whether directly or by reinforcing natural support systems. Later, crisis theory made an important contribution, and there was continuing study of the consequences of traumatic experiences at key points in the life cycle, for instance childhood, adolescence or old age, or in handicapping conditions, whether physical, psychological, economic or social. The concepts themselves were extended to include, for example, loss of a limb or of a familiar setting; and in time bereavement studies added a further dimension. A strongly developed or weak sense of identity and relations with significant others were identified as crucial to ability to surmount crises and loss. The causes of child abuse began to be clarified but little was known about how to reverse the consequences.

The importance of fathers only began to be recognised comparatively late in the period, though usable knowledge about marriage relationships increased.

In the whole period usable knowledge grew about people who were delinquent, deprived, single parents, uprooted, homeless, grossly inadequate parents, alcoholic, addicted, handicapped; or suffering from acute or chronic or terminal illness or psychiatric disorder, or bad housing, chronic poverty, or destructive relationships, or social rejection, or other damaging experiences beyond their capacity to cope successfully. Naturally there were conflicting theories about contributory causation and appropriate interdisciplinary action, and the relative significance of personal and social factors.

The rapid increase of usable sociological knowledge created a new dimension. To a considerable extent interest shifted from personal to social constituents of private sorrows and public issues as sociological studies demonstrated the effects of social attitudes and the environment on individual behaviour. These studies included social structure and institutions especially the class structure and marriage, family relationships and expectations and child-rearing practices, cultural patterns and values, social control and social conflict, social deviance, work and other roles, socialisation, social networks, and social change.

These are examples from the immense though uneven explosion of usable knowledge, knowledge that could also be applied far beyond the bounds of social work or the practice and policies of social agencies. Nonetheless social problems, urban blight and individual distress, also multiplied.

Third, *method*: "why" and "how to do". Psychoanalytically orientated casework began to spread in the 1950s partly as a result of seminars taken by visiting American social work educators, especially amongst some probation and child care officers, family caseworkers, and medical and psychiatric social workers. The method was based upon social diagnoses or assessment using such psychoanalytical concepts as early family experiences, unconscious motivation, irrational behaviour, the defence mechanisms and the powerful drives of sex and aggression. A prime tool in subsequent treatment was a "corrective emotional experience" through the relationship with the caseworker. Not all clients were motivated to form such a relationship or able to use a "talking therapy". Thus in time the insights of dynamic psychology were more widely used than a method based upon it. There were violent conflicts between those who practised and tried to extend these new methods and ways of working and those who clung to old practices based largely on personal experience.

What was indeed new — or went back to early COS principles — and remained throughout subsequent change, was systematic assessment, an attempt to identify the crucial elements in the situation and where and how to intervene, rather than engaging in superficial and ineffective activity without objectives or periodic assessment. The new methods fully recognised the powerful effect of emotions on behaviour and that to meet people's material needs could be an important element in meeting their emotional and social needs. There was also less fear about "creating dependence". Two related developments were detailed case records with a statement of goals and periodic review of "movement in the case"; and supervision, that is regular discussion with a qualified caseworker. The aim was long-term contact and substantial changes in the client's life. Obviously few caseworkers were able to carry out these methods in full.

Initially caseworkers tended to concentrate on pathology rather than strengths, to be too open-ended, diffuse and non-directive, and sometimes to overestimate the power of the casework relationship and underestimate that of the environment. In time the focus shifted and good casework became whatever form of practice most effectively met the needs of the client. This made heavier demands on the caseworker and shifted attention from childhood experiences to the current reality and how to reinforce the client's capacity to cope and the strengths of his natural support systems. The new methods demanded that the caseworker should have considerable self-awareness if he was to give an impartial service free from personal likes and dislikes. Later this was seen to include culturally based assumptions, values and prejudices.

Inevitably this wider view included the strength of family, neighbourhood, work or school relationships (whether negative or positive) and the futility of trying to change isolated individuals without taking these interactions into account. Hence more systematic attempts to lessen family stress, for example through day centres or holiday breaks, to support self-help groups, and to work through and with small groups of many different kinds. As in previous development, this was the aim, rather than common practice. Unfortunately, social group work, based on knowledge of group dynamics, was for a long while practically unknown, thus unnecessary blunders were made. Yet groups were found to be more effective than or as a reinforcement for casework in many different situations. Outstanding examples were intermediate treatment and also conscious use of group and inter-group relations in many residential, day care and community action situations.

The development in the 1970s of task-centred casework resulted from the discovery that some well-motivated clients progressed better through achieving agreed goals within a time limit (six to eight interviews). Contracts between the client and the social worker about aims began to be more widely used – and walked a tight rope between client participation and manipulation. Of course long-term (even if intermittent) casework continued to be necessary in some work with children or delinquent or old or handicapped people and their families (if any). But there too the emphasis was on periodic assessment with the client, and specific goals and intermediate objectives.

Earlier attempts to see the client apart from his family for unhurried, uninterrupted discussions became outmoded as research demonstrated the strength of the interactions within the family group and therefore that more effective change could result from the therapist working with the whole family as a group to help them to express their feelings about each other and thus to communicate and to change their perceptions. Family therapy spread rapidly in the 1970s.

Crisis intervention techniques were based on the discovery that people are more open to change in crises and will either muster better coping capacities or be damaged without the right support. This led to some attempts at quick action, for example in sudden illness or accident, bereavement or family change.

Behaviour modification, using operant conditioning through positive or negative reinforcement, began to be more generally used either on its own or as part of other techniques. There was concern among some social workers at the use of negative conditioning especially with children. But in any event positive reinforcement proved more effective.

These examples show a move away from concentration on the individual and his past to emphasis on the current situation and the interaction between individuals and their social networks. A wider range of techniques became available for differential use and in combination with each other; goals became more limited at the same time that the number of imaginative experiments increased. The boundaries between casework, group work and community work became unreal when the aim was to use whatever methods and resources might be most effective in particular circumstances.

Until the late 1960s there was little analysis of community work practice, use of social science theory or attempts at conceptualisation. Indeed, some community activists denied that this was possible without destroying their spontaneous partnership with local people. But others began to use concepts from sociology, social psychology and political theory to try to understand the forces at work in the power structure, especially government and industry, in group and inter-group relations, in rivalries and power struggles, and how to support local people in working for and carrying through self-chosen objectives. Many community workers denied that they were social workers but some others qualified on CQSW courses with a community option.

The boundaries of these methods of work with individuals, families, groups and communities became more arbitary as knowledge about interaction and the most effective method of intervention in particular circumstances increased. Interest in the integrated method gained ground – the flexible use of casework, group work and community work. The formidable practical difficulties were that the CQSW courses were too short and overloaded to give students any real competence in a wide range of skills and that social agencies still primarily used casework. The related unitary model which began to be taught on some courses faced the same difficulties. It was based on general systems theory – of social systems, including individuals and families in constant interaction with each other. The social work aim was to help people to meet their life tasks. This entailed working with four systems: the social worker himself as a change agent; the client system; the target system (which might or might not be the client system, since sometimes it is only possible to help the client by bringing about change in, for example, a school or work situation); and the action system, which was the social worker, the client and target systems and others in interaction with each other. Within this frame of reference a range of skills was necessary.

Fourth, *training*. In the 1940s the social science courses were in confusion and no one was satisfied with them. Some thought they were too academic and wanted more relevant teaching, more about social work and more practical work: others resisted this. The two obligatory practical work placements were still in family casework and settlements – where social work was pioneered. Many ex-students went into social work with no further training; the specialised courses, lasting six, nine or twelve months, some simply an apprenticeship training, were taken by people with or without a social science qualification.

In 1947 in the wake of the Curtis report four universities agreed to run one-year child care courses sponsored and financed by the Home Office's Central Training Council in Child Care (CTC). This was a welcome move into the universities but it did nothing to end specialisation, though many people thought that the essential knowledge and skill were the same in any setting. After much discussion a Carnegie Trust grant made it possible in 1954 to start the first applied social studies (generic) course at the London School of Economics for students with a social science qualification intending to become medical social workers, probation, child care officers, or "general" caseworkers. The lecture discussions were planned as a whole, while each supervisor had several students and was attached to the staff. This set a standard which was difficult to maintain as courses spread. Finally generic rather than specialised training became the accepted pattern at the basic training stage.

Meanwhile, new ideas about field work teaching struggled with old ideas about "moving students round to see all sides of the work", "making themselves useful", and "letting everyone have a go". The limelight had indeed shifted from understanding the agency to understanding the client and being able to help him. Social work teachers and supervisors with something to teach beyond their own experience were almost non-existent and had to be created. This was a revolutionary move at the time in face of resistance and inertia and because employing agencies had to be prepared for some of their best staff to give time to student supervision which tried to link theory and practice. Slowly this was taken for granted, though standards varied.

The training explosion of the 1960s would not have been possible without readily available student grants and the national and publicly financed training councils: the Advisory Council for Probation and After-Care (ACPAC); the CTC; and from 1962 the Council for Training in Social Work (CTSW) to promote training for social workers in the local authority health and welfare services. In 1961 two-year combined social studies and social work courses were started in colleges of further education. In time this addition to university courses doubled output. The National Institute for Social Work also did much from the 1960s to advance social work education and practice.

Trained social workers and courses were concentrated in a few parts of the country, so the three training councils made great efforts to spread training to desert areas. This meant initiating in-service training courses and fresh appointments to try to bring up local standards for student supervision and teaching. In time qualifying courses covered the whole country. The problem of how to increase numbers and at the same time raise standards was acute. Pleas for centres of excellence were not heeded in pressure for more output, but educational qualifications were raised and in time universities started post-graduate master's degree courses; it was also assumed that social work teachers would undertake research. Unfortunately in the rush to expand basic training post-qualifying courses were almost non-existent until the mid-1970s.

At first teaching was confined to casework but group work and community work began to be added in some courses and later a few concentrated on the unitary model.

In-service training began in the 1940s through a few small courses run by professional associations. Later, the training councils sponsored short courses all over the country for hundreds of social workers each year and finally employing bodies appointed training officers. The effect of widespread in-service training, and indeed of agency policy, in raising standards has unfortunately never been studied.

From the start the CTC ran one-year courses in residential child care. Much time was given to home-making skills and the courses were on a lower educational level than those for field workers. In the late 1960s the new concept of residential social work resulted in attempts to introduce a residential stream in some social work courses. It became official policy that some staff in any residential care establishment should be qualified in residential social work. But unfortunately there was always a shortage of candidates, even when the staff were non-resident.

In 1971 the statutory Central Council for Education and Training in Social Work (CCETSW) superceded the three separate publicly financed councils. It faced the problem of bringing over 120 courses on various patterns up to a common minimum standard and it substituted the one certificate of qualification in social work (CQSW) for all courses which it recognised. The battle to increase numbers continued and in the 1970s thousands qualified each year against a handful in the 1950s. All basic courses became generic and the struggles of the medical and psychiatric social workers to increase their numbers without adequate resources ceased when they became part of BASW. It became clear that the personal social services needed a variety of trained staff in addition to qualified social workers. These included home help organisers, assistants in day care and residential centres, and teachers of the mentally handicapped. CCETSW accepted responsibility for training some staff other than social workers and instituted the certificate in social service (CSS) to give a shorter and more technical training to these and other staff.

In the training revolution people at first only discussed what subjects to teach in the new courses. But from the early 1960s some began to think about the objectives of courses, what students must know and be able to do to qualify and thus what it was essential to teach, at what depth in both theory and practice. This included the other dimension of how students learn, how to teach, together with much discussion and some action about training the trainers. When audio-visual aids became widely available they added a powerful aid to skill learning, communication and awareness of self and others.

In summary: the additions to usable knowledge and social work methods between the 1950s and 1970s transformed social work training and practice. A new range of discontents and disagreements emerged which may prove as constructive as similar ones 30 or more years ago.

Fifth, *organisational structure and procedures*. From the 1930s the Home Office took responsibility for providing trained probation officers to match demand. In 1947 it also did so for the child care service. Coupled with local education authority training grants, this was a change from assuming that people should pay for a training that gave them a career to assuming that it was a public responsibility to provide trained manpower. This also entailed forecasting demand.

Advisory councils were a device which at its best kept government departments in touch with informed opinion, cushioned some controversial decision making, and secured expert consultation without payment.

New initiative in voluntary agency and local authority partnership and grant-aid enabled each to contribute expertise and information to the other, a wider range of resources became available, and while voluntary organisations could experiment more easily with local authority help, the latter did not burn its fingers if things went wrong but benefited if they did not.

Government and trust grants for research, coupled with much expanded university research resources, made possible the tremendous increase in social research. After 1971 the social services departments also had their own research and development units. Information about research findings was also easily available but making use of research was a different matter.

Modern technology also made possible the collection of complex data required by the new large-scale services. These services with their bureaucratic structures, multi-functional staffs and problems of determining priorities made management studies and expertise essential. These included objectives and priority ranking, monitoring, determining cost-effectiveness, staff policies, the deployment of social work and other staff, training, accountability, manpower planning, decisions about resources and experiments, budgeting, communication up as well as down, decision-making authority, relations with government departments and other related organisations and between staff and the governing body – in short all aspects of policy making, implementation and change. There were also problems of the most effective creation and use of teamwork, of area teams or "patch" systems, of consultation and specialisation, of interdisciplinary co-operation, of how to reconcile professional judgment with bureaucratic procedures, of tensions between local offices and headquarters, and between different organisations.

The emphasis on community care showed the range of resources necessary to make this effective and social work as only one element in it. These resources included home helps, meals on wheels, holiday breaks, day centres and clubs for old or physically or mentally handi-capped people, sheltered workshops, day nurseries, play centres, information and welfare rights centres, temporary accommodation, hostels, assorted lodgings, family advice centres, and other support services like drop-in centres or "phone-ins" for those at risk, including overburdened families. Skilled assessment and monitoring was necessary to use these resources effectively alone or in combination with each other and with social work counselling if necessary.

Sixth, *social care*. As a result of more knowledge about common human needs, social care had spread far beyond the bounds of social work and the personal social services and became part of the practice of other professions and services.

It first became clear in relation to the basic needs of children through-out their childhood and raised many problems of how to support ailing families or to provide good substitute care. It spread slowly and unevenly to adolescents, the sick and disabled, drop-outs, offenders, drug addicts, battered wives and abused children, alcoholics, old people and the dying. It began to permeate life in institutions like hospitals, homes for the chronic sick and the old, community homes, borstals and even prisons as well as life in the community.

Institutional neurosis was identified and the concept of the thera-peutic community with full mutual participation of residents and staff began to counter the effect on people of life in total institutions.

Self-government, self-help groups and active involvement of clients in decision-making and the service they received were means of enabling people to grow in their social relationships. Social work objectives aimed to sustain natural support systems as well as to take preventive action to forestall dangers of alienation or isolation through falling out of social life, whether as homeless adolescents or isolated old people. The notion of after-care was expanded to continuity of care — getting into the picture when prevention or support was possible, and remaining available or active whether the person was in the community or an institution.

The gap between what was known about social care and what was applied, tested and extended was only bridged in some experimental and other institutions.

Conclusion

The three periods were all distinct from each other and maybe the lost time in the middle stage was an inevitable part of the process. The search for identity has been a chief driving force in each period. The explosion of knowledge of the past 25 years, the wide range of practice, the clash of ideologies, the growth of the personal social services, the acceptance of social work, the expansion of training in both courses and content, the changed public expectations, the statutory responsibilities, and the senior appointments in large bureaucratic organisations have all come too rapidly to be absorbed. In consequence social work is commonly said to have lost its boundaries and its sense of direction, not to be clear about its function or its effectiveness, torn by conflict about its aims and methods and failing to encompass a range from politically radical social workers to those who campaign to improve clinical practice.

There have been blind spots, failures to champion social reform, rigidities and ideological dissent at each stage, too great an emphasis on either the individual or society rather than on the interaction between them, too little research — perhaps too little curiosity — within social work itself. Yet from the perspective of history the gains may outweigh faltering and failures, in any event not unique to social work. At least social workers have always been sensitive to the needs of the underdog, even if they, like others, have seen too few of them and underrated their needs.

This brief history must stop, so to speak, in the middle of a sentence, with no answer to the question whether social work will continue to tear itself apart or whether it will recover from its indigestion, consolidate its gains and find a more secure identity.

Bibliography

H Barnett, *Canon Barnett*. John Murray. 1921.

The Calouste Gulbenkian Foundation, *Community Work and Social Change*. Longman. 1968.

P Hall, *The Social Services of Modern England*. Routledge & Kegan Paul. 1952. (Subsequent editions by A Forder.)

P Hall, *Reforming the Welfare*. Allen & Unwin. 1977.

J Manton, *Mary Carpenter and the Children of the Streets*. Heinemann. 1976.

E Moberley Bell, *Octavia Hill*. Constable. 1942.

M Richmond, *Social Diagnosis*. Russell Sage Foundation. 1917.

M Roof, *A Hundred Years of Family Welfare*. Michael Joseph. 1972.

Seebohm committee, *Report of the Committee on Local Authority and Allied Social Services* (Cmnd 2703). HMSO. 1968.

P Seed, *The Expansion of Social Work in Britain*. Routledge & Kegan Paul. 1973.

M Smith, *Professional Education for Social Work in Britain*. Allen & Unwin. 1965.

J Stroud, *Thirteen Penny Stamps*. Hodder & Stoughton. 1971.

G Wagner, *Barnardo*. Weidenfeld & Nicholson. 1979.

R G Walton, *Women in Social Work*. Routledge & Kegan Paul. 1975

B Webb, *My Apprenticeship*. Penguin. 1974.

K Woodroofe, *From Charity to Social Work*. Routledge & Kegan Paul. 1962.

M Yelloly, *Social Work Theory and Psychoanalysis*. Van Norstrand & Reinhold. 1980.

A F Young and E T Ashton, *British Social Work in the Nineteeth Century*. Routledge & Kegan Paul. 1956.

E Younghusband, *Social Work in Britain: 1950–1975*. Allen & Unwin. 1978.

Editorial note

Dame Eileen Younghusband served for little more than two years as an editorial adviser to Community Care before her death in May 1981. Her association with the magazine was strengthened further when, in 1979, she joined the editorial advisory board of the series of research monographs published jointly by the magazine and the Joint Unit for Social Services Research, Sheffield University.

It was during this time that she was asked to write a short history of social work and, setting about her task with her customary dispatch and assiduity, the manuscript was in its editor's hands before she left to visit the United States where she was to meet her tragic death.

This volume concludes with the two following contributions which first appeared in the June 8 and 16 issues, respectively, of the magazine. The former, which is published in a slightly extended version than originally, is a personal tribute on behalf of the magazine by its editor. The second is also by a friend – Kathleen Jones, professor of social work and social administration, York University – but one who is also privileged to be Dame Eileen's authorised biographer.

The good companion

Terry Philpot

I t was a cruel irony that Dame Eileen should die in a road accident. No typical septugenarian would be driving to an airport in North Carolina to catch a plane to Chicago as part of a month-long visit to the United States. But then Dame Eileen was no typical septugenarian. Indeed, she was not typically anything, but her own unique self, and her death marks not just the end of an era in British social work and social policy, but the disappearance from the scene of one who, perhaps more than any other individual, did so much to shape that era.

I only came to know Dame Eileen at the very end of her life and her formal association with the magazine was a too short one: a contributor almost since its early days, she became an editorial adviser in March 1979, one of the judges in our annual travel scholarship competition and joined me, with others, as a member of the editorial board of the social services research monographs series, published jointly by *Community Care* and Sheffield University. But what she was in old age was very much what I imagine her to have been throughout her life — stimulating, energetic to a point where she put those 40 or .50 years her junior to shame, and endlessly active.

She was not, in what one can hardly describe with any truth as retirement, one of those elderly people whom she once described society as making "marginal people to be sentimental about". She had come into social work in her 20s when a friend impressed upon her the need for what she called a purpose in life. Fortunately, that sense never diminished, and, if anything, seemed to increase with the years. In fact, writing nearly four years ago she said: "The great recipe for young old age is to have an aim to live for, an aim that transcends the 'long littleness of every day'." ("Is old age a good age?" *Community Care*, 7 December 1977.)

What she prescribed there was very much from the experience of her own then 76 years. "The challenge is for old people to be enabled to discover new outlets for their energies, new or altered ways of living that satisfy them and through which they are fulfilled in some pursuit, jointly with relatives, friends or a group of like-minded people, giving and receiving in open-ended not dead-end activities. I mean by open-ended those activities which lead onto some further result. There is no neat recipe for this and it may take very different forms from growing and giving away cabbages to becoming another Grandma Moses."

I don't know that, strictly speaking, Dame Eileen discovered *new* outlets for she continued to be active in social work from 1924, when she went to work in South London and the East End, until her death, and although jobs came and went, her profession changed and developed, her life conformed to no arbitrary cordons of time. In her 70s, for example, she embarked upon an updating of her two major Carnegie Trust reports *(Employment and Training of Social Workers 1946); Social work in Great Britain 1951)*, which emerged in 1978 as *Social Work in Britain: 1950-1975*, a massive, two volume, comprehensive survey. She fondly referred to this work as "the albatross" because the original task had grown and grown. She even suggested — well, she said, "may be", which allowed her not to carry out her intentions — that when it was finished she might buy a television set and settle down to read who-dun-its, novels and biographies that she had wished she had had time for.

The depth of her experience but also the enviable perspective that was her's came home when I was editing the manuscript of this monograph. I was arrogant and foolish enough to suggest an expansion of certain developments in the last decade or so. In return I quite properly received the mildest of reproofs to the effect that she would consider my suggestions, "remembering that what happens today is no more important than what happened a hundred years ago". Thus it was, too, that she was anxious that in selecting photographs no suggestion was given that a dark age had given way to a period of undiluted enlightenment — poverty, bad housing and want still existed, even if they wore different faces.

Her 80 years, of course, offered a companion an endless source of fascination. One year the essay competition judges met in the Piccadilly Hotel, and as she stepped inside she said with obvious affection: "I haven't been here for a hundred years and it hasn't changed at all". She then proceeded to describe the London of carriages and the horse-drawn buses and supper and dinner with one's friends. At lunch one of us mentioned a grandfather who had fought at the Somme. Utterly matter-of-factly and with no wish to impress, but only to interest, Dame Eileen chipped in with: "I had an uncle, you know, who fought in the Crimea."

Her experience, knowledge and perspective was ever useful in her capacity as an editorial adviser. The meetings were always enlivened by her suggestions and her wit and one liked to think that she had a soft spot for the magazine ("Some indication of how *Community Care* began and developed. May its shadow never grow less", reads an inscription by her in a copy of her history). Her personal interest in the travel scholarship, the acuity with which she read the essays and the shrewdness and originality of her judgements was a mark of her eager interest in encouraging young, and especially student, social workers.

I can never remember her turning down any request, large or small, and the fact that she was a regular speaker at courses and conferences indicated that advancing age was no deterrent. Her globe-trotting was daunting – last year she visited Switzerland and the United States, and a dozen other places for all one knows. She was also a participant at the International Association of Schools of Social Work congress in Hong Kong. A consultant many years past to the Hong Kong government in establishing its social work training programmes, she was greeted by the Chinese as a mixture of guru and favourite aunt returned home. There are many there who will remember with amusement her checking out of the luxurious Mandarin Hotel for the more convenient and homely YWCA.

Her vast experience had been drawn upon in latter years by other countries. Interviewed in 1976, she said that in July of that year she had attended an international workshop in Jamaica, a conference on social welfare in Puerto Rico and had visited Washington.

It was not easy to imagine that this was the same person who 60 years before began her social work in London's East End. A little later she had gone to live in the Princess Club Settlement, Bermondsey, and recounted how, despite being regarded as "the peel around the onion", the lowest form of life, tea was brought in by a maid each morning.

Her life began in the era of the soup kitchens and the workhouse and ended in the welfare state and modern generic social work training – which her reports had recommended more than 30 years ago – available within and without the universities, another achievement that can be put at her door. It was, indeed, in the words of the title of Kathleen Woodroofe's history, a life spanning "from charity to social work".

Perhaps it was this perspective that allowed her not to be depressed at social work's meanderings. She once said that perhaps social work had to lose its way to find itself.

This is not the place to describe her manifold contribution to academic life and social work. Those who knew her – and she numbered her friends by the dozen, the length of friendships often in terms of decades, with national frontiers no boundary – will miss the sheer zest and enthusiasm, wisdom, humour and relish for friendship of one who, despite her years and her physical slightness, seemed, in a way, the least destructible of persons.

One anecdote, then, to sum up her impish humour and also her humility. She was attending her local BASW branch meeting in the months before her death and one young and inexperienced social worker, not knowing who she was, came up, introduced herself and asked Dame Eileen her name. This made no impact and her companion then asked what she had done. Unabashed, the reply was that she had done a little bit here and there in NISW and the training field.

42

A capacity for living

Kathleen Jones

E ileen Younghusband was so much part of the social work scene that is is difficult to realise that she is gone. Next January would have seen her 80th birthday, and she was already looking forward to a celebration at the London School of Economics, which would have brought together many of her old friends and colleagues in her honour. Last summer found her at the International Association of Schools of Social Work Congress in Hong Kong, active and engaged as ever, and reaching out to new friendships and new experiences. She was particularly excited by a brief trip across the border into China. Perhaps it was fitting that the end of her life came in action – on one of her many trips to the United States, in a car accident as she left the University of North Carolina at Chapel Hill to catch a plane for Chicago. Though she grew old with grace and patience, there was a sense in which she never grew old at all.

In British social work, Eileen will be remembered chiefly for her many years of teaching at LSE; for the two Carnegie reports, which mapped out the state of social work after the Second World War; for the Younghusband report of 1959 (which she always insisted on referring to in full – the report of the Committee on Social Workers in the Local Authority Health and Welfare Services, rather than attaching her own name to it); for her work as chairman of a juvenile court; for her part as consultant and adviser to the National Institute of Social Work Training, as it then was, in the 1960s; and for her editing and writing, notably the two-volume *Social Work in Britain 1950-75*, published as recently as 1978. These are the high-lights; behind them lies a long and full life of committee work, of report writing, of lucid thought and purposeful activity in the interests of the social work profession.

When Eileen undertook the first study for the Carnegie United Kingdom Trust – the report on the Employment and Training of Social Workers (1947) – social work was fragmented, and training chaotic. Eighteen universities offered courses in social science or social study, but only five of these made any mention of the principles and methods of social work in their prospectuses. Training was highly academic, with fieldwork tacked on as a necessary but unintegrated extra. Professional training was achieved only by a few, and this had a very small academic content. The prestigious training offered by the Institute of Almoners had no examination, and it was "possible for a student to go through the whole of her final year without writing a paper". Probation training suffered from "the poor educational standard of many applicants", and psychiatric social workers were a

43

tiny minority inhabiting a private professional world of their own. Social workers were mainly women — "like cats" noted Eileen, rather obscurely — badly paid, overworked, and lacking a sense of common professional identity. The report set out with precision and clarity the range of tasks covered by social workers, the gaps, overlaps and anomalies in training. The salary scales, the expectations of employers, and the lack of support services. She noted that "a trained social worker [will] start at the same salary as a good shorthand-typist, but it may well be that some thorough job analyses . . . would reveal her doing a variety of things which the shorthand-typist would expect to delegate to the office girl". Her recommendations included the setting up of an experimental school of social work which would train students for work in a variety of settings, teaching the core of social work theory and practice which was already being taught in American schools of social work, and which she saw as necessary to the setting up of a single profession in Britain. It would be concerned with both education *and* training — Eileen's emphasis on the necessity of integrating theoretical knowledge and practice knowledge, and of developing "a theory of practice" was central to her approach, and is now reflected in the title of the Central Council for Education and Training in Social Work. It would need a research arm — "research would be the life-blood of the school". There would be post-qualification courses for multi-disciplinary groups, and facilities for study for social workers from other countries.

Four years later, Eileen produced her second Carnegie report, charting the many changes which had occurred in the immediate post-war period. The creation of new and improved social services in the welfare state legislation had led to an improved status for social workers — "due, no doubt, to the war-time discovery of officialdom that a trained social worker in an awkward, difficult or tangled situation could help to bring order out of chaos and light into darkness". Salaries and conditions had improved, demand had increased, and more men were coming into social work; but the basic problems remained — the gap between theory and practice, the need to define social work in relation to the work of doctors, health visitors and teachers, the need for research, the need for co-ordination. If some of these problems have a modern ring about them, and we still do not know all the answers, we need to recognise how very far we have travelled since 1951, and how much of the impetus has come from Eileen's work. The two reports combine an encyclopaedic knowledge of the subject with a remarkable grasp of administrative procedure, and a vision of what social work was capable of becoming.

After protracted negotiations, the Carnegie course was set up at LSE under Eileen's direction. Professor Charlotte Towle came over from Chicago to help launch it, and the scheme, which involved extensive contacts with field agencies in London and supervisors' courses, ran on an experimental basis for three years, side by side with the mental health course and the new child care course. Then came the question of merging the three courses into a generic applied social studies course, the first of its kind. Paradoxically Eileen, who had done so much for the development of social work, was not technically a qualified social worker – and by this time, qualification mattered. The professional groups had been pursuing their own road to unity through the Standing Conference of Social Work Organisations, and the course was judged (probably rightly in the context of the time) to need professional leadership.

Eileen left LSE and devoted her energies to promoting social work in public life. She was already involved in what the rest of the social work world called the Younghusband committee. To Eileen's disappointment, the committee's terms of reference covered only social workers in the local authority health and welfare services, not the whole spectrum of social work. Even so, its report was a document which was to have profound effects on social work training. Its recommendations led to the setting up of "Younghusband" two-year training courses outside the universities, and hence to a rapid expansion in the numbers of social workers; to the employment of welfare assistants; to considerable improvements in conditions of work in local government departments; and to the setting up of NISW.

Eileen threw her energies into the National Institute – planning, teaching and organising in close consultation with the first principal, Robin Huws Jones, and into advising the new (what was then called) Council for Training in Social Work. The task of developing a new cadre of social workers, of devising courses and teaching the teachers, of monitoring their practice and employment conditions, was a massive one. Without that work, and Eileen's unique combination of tireless committee work and personal inspiration, the basis would have been lacking for the Seebohm report and the Local Authority Social Services Act of 1971.

Looking back, it all makes a pattern in Eileen's life – the vision of the late 1940s, the experimental and exciting 1950s, the achievement of the 1960s with the DBE in 1964, and the reflective consolidation of the 1970s, when the stream of social work development had passed into other hands. But the development of social work in Britain is only one aspect of a full and varied life. While she has recorded that story in her two volumes published in 1978 in her usual meticulous and pragmatic style, she was equally active in the international scene. She produced major reports on social work training in India and Hong Kong, carried out consultancies in Greece and Turkey and East and West Africa and the West Indies, and visited many parts of the world in connection with the International Association of Schools of Social Work. Wherever she went, there were friends to see and colleagues to listen to and advise, and young people who crowded round her to catch something of the vision and the dynamic she represented. Though instinctively reserved in her personal life, she could reach out across the barriers of race and age and social class with genuine warmth and understanding.

Eileen came from a privileged background. Her father, Sir Francis Younghusband, was a distinguished mountaineer and explorer, and the story of his expedition to Tibet is almost legendary. Her mother, who insisted on her "coming out" and doing the round of London society for some years, had difficulty in understanding a daughter who wanted to spend her life in the London School of Economics and the back streets of Bermondsey and Stepney, where she did settlement work for some years. Eileen made friends with the factory girls, and knew their lives — the effects of sickness, malnutrition and poverty, the dirty, raucous tenements, the perilous finances that took them from the pawnshop to the jumble sale, the funerals, the street fights, the drunkenness and the sheer grind of survival. Though she was generous and hospitable to her friends, a kind of personal frugality clung to her from those days, and served her well when she went on to face the problems of the developing countries. She had an acute sense of social injustice, and an instinct to serve.

A few people (mostly British, and mostly in senior positions) were rather afraid of her. Her tough, incisive mind could not tolerate shoddy or half-formed thinking, and she could puncture pomposity quicker than most. Truth had to be served, and an intense honesty made her very direct in her judgements. A highly effective chairman, she would use all her committee skills and her administrative skills to get her points across, and to ensure that they were translated into action; but she was also very kind, and capable of great gentleness in friendship. The factory girls of her early settlement days, children and parents in the juvenile court, bright students and the not so bright, social workers of any nationality, trained, half-trained or untrained, found in her a simplicity and capacity for fun sometimes hidden from her colleagues.

Eileen loved learning, and she learned both from books and from life. There was a time when as a student, she sat down in the garden in her family home at Westerham in Kent with McDougall's *Principles of Psychology* in the expectation that, when she had finished it, she would know all about human behaviour. The analysis of instinct, perception and conation disappointed her. She was to note in the second Carnegie report (though not *à propos* of McDougall) that "it is a matter of common observation that persons of high intelligence can be very boring". She believed that social work was an important means of combating personal misery and social inequality; that a social worker's chief tool was his or her own personality, and that good education and training, based on sound principles and humane values, could make that work more effective. She believed that social workers needed to develop "a capacity for living" in order to stimulate in their clients' healing and growth. She had that capacity herself, and she used it to the full.